52 Ear

D0404238

From the publishers of **Bead&Button**, **Bead Style**, and **Art Jewelry** magazines

Fast
Fashionable
&Fun

KB
KALMBACH BOOKS

Kalmbach Books
21027 Crossroads Circle
Waukesha, Wisconsin 53186
www.Kalmbach.com/Books

Published in 2012
16 15 14 13 12   1 2 3 4 5

Manufactured in the United States of America

ISBN: 978-0-87116-712-5

The material in this book has appeared previously in *Bead Style* magazine and the *Under $25, BeadStyle Around the World, Your Perfect Look, Crystals,* and *Pearls* special issues. *Bead Style* is registered as a trademark.

Editor: *Elisa Neckar*
Technical Editor: *Karin Van Voorhees*
Art Director: *Lisa Bergman*
Designers: *Mike Soliday & Tom Ford*
Proofreader: *Erica Swanson*
Photographers: *Bill Zuback & Jim Forbes*

Library of Congress Cataloging-in-Publication Data
52 earrings / from the publishers of Bead&Button, BeadStyle, and Art Jewelry magazines.

   p. : ill. (chiefly col.) ; cm.

   "Fast, fashionable & fun."
   "The material in this book has appeared previously in BeadStyle magazine and the Under $25, BeadStyle Around the World, Your Perfect Look, Crystals, and Pearls special issues."–T.p. verso.
   ISBN: 978-0-87116-712-5

   1. Earrings–Handbooks, manuals, etc. 2. Beadwork–Handbooks, manuals, etc. 3. Jewelry making–Handbooks, manuals, etc. I. Kalmbach Publishing Company. II. Title: Fifty-two earrings III. Title: BeadStyle Magazine.

TT860 .F54 2012
745.594/2

Contents

Basics

Plain loop

1 Trim the wire ⅜ in. (1cm) above the top bead. Make a right-angle bend close to the bead.
2 Grab the wire's tip with roundnose pliers. Roll the wire to form a half circle.
3 Reposition the pliers in the loop and continue rolling, forming a centered circle above the bead.
4 The finished loop.

Wrapped loop

1 Make sure there is at least 1¼ in. (3.2cm) of wire above the bead. With the tip of your chainnose pliers, grasp the wire directly above the bead. Bend the wire (above the pliers) into a right angle.
2 Position the jaws of your roundnose pliers vertically in the bend.
3 Bring the wire over the pliers' top jaw.
4 Reposition the pliers' lower jaw snugly in the curved wire. Wrap the wire down and around the bottom of the pliers. This is *the first half of a wrapped loop.*
5 Grasp the loop with chainnose pliers.
6 Wrap the wire tail around the wire stem, covering the stem between the loop and the top bead. Trim the excess wrapping wire, and press the end close to the stem with chainnose or crimping pliers.

Making a set of wraps above a top-drilled bead

1 Center a top-drilled bead on a 3-in. (7.6cm) piece of wire. Bend each end upward, crossing the wires into an X.
2 Using chainnose pliers, make a small bend in each wire to form a right angle.
3 Wrap the horizontal wire around the vertical wire as in a wrapped loop. Trim the excess wrapping wire.

Cutting memory wire

Memory wire is hardened steel, so it will dent and ruin the jaws of most wire cutters. Use heavy-duty wire cutters, cutters specifically designed for memory wire, or bend the wire back and forth until it snaps.

Opening a jump ring or loop

1 Hold the jump ring or loop with chainnose and roundnose pliers or two pairs of chainnose pliers.
2 To open the jump ring or loop, bring one pair of pliers toward you.
3 The open jump ring. Reverse the steps to close.

Flattened crimp

1 Hold the crimp bead with the tip of your chainnose pliers. Squeeze the pliers firmly to flatten the crimp bead. Tug the clasp to make sure the crimp has a solid grip on the wire. If the wire slides, remove the crimp bead and repeat with a new crimp bead.
2 The flattened crimp.

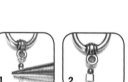

Folded crimp

1 Position the crimp bead in the notch closest to the crimping pliers' handle.
2 Separate the wires and firmly squeeze the crimp bead.
3 Move the crimp bead into the notch at the pliers' tip. Squeeze the pliers, folding the bead in half at the indentation.
4 The folded crimp.

Folded crimp end

1 Glue one end of the cord and place it in a crimp end. Use chainnose pliers to fold one side of the crimp end over the cord.
2 Repeat with the second side of the crimp end and squeeze gently.

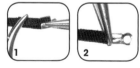

Overhand knot

Make a loop and pass the working end through it. Pull the ends to tighten the knot.

Tools & Materials

Most beaded jewelry projects, including those in this book, require some combination of chainnose, roundnose, and crimping pliers, as well as diagonal wire cutters. These four tools should be your first investment when you begin beading, and should be kept close at hand as you make projects from this book. Other tools, such as the hammer, will be used only with specific projects. Use the tools as directed in the project instructions and Basics section to complete your jewelry.

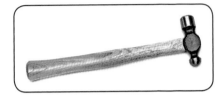

A **hammer** is used to harden and texture wire. Any hammer with a flat head will work, as long as the head is free of nicks that could mar your metal. The light ball-peen hammer shown here is one of the most commonly used hammers for jewelry making.

Chainnose pliers have smooth, flat inner jaws, and the tips taper to a point. Use them for gripping and for opening and closing loops and jump rings.

Roundnose pliers have smooth, tapered, conical jaws used to make loops. The closer to the tip you work, the smaller the loop will be.

A **bench block** provides a hard, smooth surface on which to hammer your pieces. An anvil is similarly hard but has different surfaces, such as a tapered horn, to help form wire into different shapes.

Crimping pliers have two grooves in their jaws that are used to fold or roll a crimp bead into a compact shape.

With **diagonal wire cutters**, use the front of the blades to make a pointed cut and the back of the blades to make a flat cut.

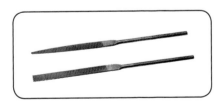

Metal files are used to refine and shape the edges of metal and wire surfaces.

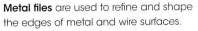

Start with beads and findings...

Beads come in an incredible range of colors, shapes, and sizes, and are made from a variety of materials, including crystals and glass, gemstones, pearls and shells, metals, and wood and other natural materials.

Findings like filigree components, spacers, cones, and connectors let you connect and position the elements of your jewelry, or may even serve as the main focal point.

Choose your stringing materials...

A **head pin** looks like a long, thick, blunt sewing pin. It has a flat or decorative head on one end to keep the beads in place. Head pins come in different diameters, or gauges, and lengths ranging from 1–3 in. (2.5–7.6cm). Eye pins have a round loop at one end rather than a head.

Flexible beading wire is composed of steel wires twisted together and covered with nylon.

Wire is available in a number of materials and finishes — brass, gold, gold-filled, gold-plated, fine silver, sterling silver, anodized niobium (chemically colored wire), and copper — and in varying hardnesses and shapes. Wire thickness is measured by gauge; the higher the gauge, the thinner the wire.

Cord and other fibers are alternative stringing options; ensure that the holes in your beads are large enough for the cord to pass through, as most fibers are thicker than beading wire.

Chain is available in many finishes (sterling silver, gold-filled, base metal, plated metal) and styles (curb, figaro, long-and-short, rolo, cable). Often chain links can be opened in the same way loops and jump rings are opened.

Assemble your earrings...

Crimp beads are small, large-holed, thin-walled metal beads designed to be flattened or crimped into a tight roll. A crimp bead cover closes over the crimp, mimicking the look of a small bead.

Crimp ends and **pinch ends** are used to connect the ends of leather, ribbons, or other fiber lacing materials.

A **jump ring** is used to connect two components. It is a small wire circle or oval that is either soldered or comes with an opening.

Earring findings come in a variety of metals, and in styles including post, French hook, lever-back, earring thread, and hoop. You will almost always want a loop (or loops) on earring findings so you can attach beads.

Stacked pearls

Jane Konkel

Supplies

- **2** 10mm pearls
- **2** 8mm pearls
- **2** 6mm pearls
- **2** 4mm pearls
- **2** 2-in. (5cm) head pins
- pair of earring wires

1 On a head pin, string: 10mm pearl, 8mm pearl, 6mm pearl, 4mm pearl. Make a wrapped loop (Basics).

2 Open the loop of an earring wire (Basics) and attach the dangle. Close the loop. Make a second earring.

Cathy Jakicic

Cathy Jakicic

● **Design alternatives**
Use the same technique to stack seed beads and crystals on a head pin, or attach a second bead-filled head pin to your earring wire for dual dangles.

A pop of pearls

Monica Han

Supplies

- ◆ **2** 10mm crystal pearls
- ◆ **2** 27mm hammered rings
- ◆ **2** 24mm hammered rings
- ◆ 6 in. (15cm) 22-gauge half-hard wire
- ◆ pair of earring wires

1 Cut a 3-in. (7.6cm) piece of wire. Make the first half of a wrapped loop (Basics) large enough to accommodate the rings. String a 10mm pearl. Make the first half of a wrapped loop.

2 Attach a 27mm ring and a 24mm ring to the loop and complete all wraps.

3 Open the loop of an earring wire (Basics). Attach the dangle and close the loop. Make a second earring.

Around the bend

Jess DiMeo

Supplies

- **2** 1-in. (2.5cm) curved silver tube beads
- **2** 8mm round beads
- **4** 2–3mm round spacers
- **8 in. (20cm) 20-gauge half-hard wire
- metal file

1 Cut a 4-in. (10cm) piece of wire. Bend it in half. On one end, string a curved-tube bead, a spacer, an 8mm bead, and a spacer.

2 Make a plain loop (Basics). File the other end of the wire. Make a second earring.

● **Design alternative** For a dressier pair of earrings, try gold tube beads with filigree rounds and 12mm crystal pearls.

● **Tip**

Leave a small space between the tube and the bend so the tube doesn't poke your ear.

Thanks a bunch

Camilla Jorgensen

Supplies

- ◆ **42–54** 5–6mm button pearls
- ◆ 3 in. (7.6cm) cable chain, 1mm links
- ◆ **42–54** 1-in. (2.5cm) decorative head pins
- ◆ **2** 3–4mm jump rings
- ◆ pair of earring posts with ear nuts

1 On a decorative head pin, string a pearl and make a plain loop (Basics). Make 21 to 27 pearl units.

2 Cut a 1½-in. (3.8cm) piece of chain. Open the loop of a pearl unit (Basics) and attach an end link of the chain. Close the loop. Attach two pearl units to the next link. Repeat, alternating one and two units per link, leaving about ½ in. (1.3cm) of the chain open at the top. Use a jump ring to attach the chain to the earring post. Make a second earring.

● **Design alternative**
Try using old-fashioned shoe buttons instead of pearls. The buttons come with premade loops.

Draped drama

Brenda Schweder

Supplies

- ◆ **4–6** 5mm or 6mm bicone crystals
- ◆ **4–6** 3mm bicone crystals
- ◆ **8–10** 4mm cube crystals
- ◆ 16 in. (41cm) cable chain, 3–4mm links
- ◆ 11 in. (28cm) figaro chain, 3–4mm links
- ◆ **16–22** 1-in. (2.5cm) head pins
- ◆ **16–20** 3–4mm inside diameter jump rings
- ◆ pair of hoop earrings with loops

1 On a head pin, string a crystal. Make a plain loop (Basics). Make eight to 11 crystal units.

2 Cut a 5-in. (13cm) piece of figaro chain. Open a jump ring (Basics) and attach an end link of chain and a hoop earring's loop. Close the jump ring. Repeat at the other end.

3 Use jump rings to attach the chain to other loops on the earring finding, draping the chain as desired.

4 Cut an 8-in. (20cm) piece of cable chain. Use jump rings to attach the chain to the earring as desired.

5 Open the loop of a crystal unit. Attach it to a chain link or to a loop of the earring. Close the loop. Attach the remaining crystal units to the earring as desired. Make a second earring.

Branching out

Georgia Hadley

Supplies

- ◆ **6** 3–5mm beads
- ◆ **6** 1½-in. (3.8cm) 24-gauge head pins
- ◆ pair of earrings wires
- ◆ mandrel or other cylindrical object, 15mm in diameter

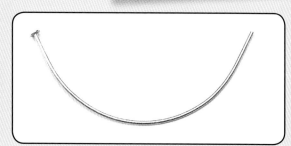

1 Bend a head pin around the cylindrical object. Make a total of three curved head pins.

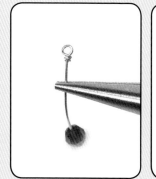

2 String a bead on a curved head pin. Make a small (2 to 3mm) wrapped loop (Basics) ½ to ¾ in. (1.3 to 2cm) from the bead.

3 String a bead on a second curved head pin, then go through the wrapped loop on the previous head pin. Make sure the head pins curve in opposite directions. Make a small wrapped loop ½ to ¾ in. from the bead.

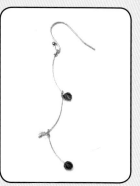

4 Repeat step 3 with a third curved head pin. Open the loop on an earring wire and attach the dangle. Close the loop. Make a second earring.

Pretty petals

Lindsay Burke

Supplies

- ♦ **2** 16–19mm crystal pendants
- ♦ **1g** 11º seed beads
- ♦ **8** 4–5mm crystals
- ♦ **12 in.** (30cm) 26-gauge wire
- ♦ pair of earring wires

1 Cut a 6-in. (15cm) piece of wire. Center eight 11º seed beads, a pendant, and eight 11ºs. Twist the wires together next to the seed beads.

2 On one wire (B), string 18 11ºs. Make a loop, tightening the wire so there's no space between the beads, and wrap the wire twice around the other wire (A).

3 On wire B, string a 4–5mm crystal. Bring the wire across the crystal and wrap it twice around wire A.

4 Repeat steps 2 and 3 with wire A. Switch wires and repeat steps 2 and 3 again. If you want a fourth leaf, repeat step 2 using either wire.

5 String a crystal over both wires. Twist the wires together for at least 1¼ in. (3.2cm). Make a wrapped loop (Basics) with the twisted wires.

6 Open the loop of an earring wire (Basics). Attach the dangle and close the loop. Make a second earring.

Hoops of fire

Lindsay Mikulsky

Supplies

- ◆ **14** 3–4mm faceted rondelles
- ◆ **12** 4mm flat spacers
- ◆ 6 in. (15cm) 24-gauge half-hard wire
- ◆ metal file

1 Cut a 3-in. (7.6cm) piece of wire. Wrap it around an empty spool or other round object.

2 String an alternating pattern of seven rondelles and six spacers. Center the beads on the wire.

Jessica Tiemens

● **Design alternative** Try curving your wire into shapes other than a simple hoop, as in this elongated drop.

3 Approximately ⅛ in. (3mm) from one end, bend the wire up. File the end.

4 On the other end, make a plain loop (Basics). Make a second earring.

Organic design

Irina Miech

Supplies
- **12** 8–12mm large-hole pearls
- 42-in. (1.1m) silk ribbon
- pair of earring wires

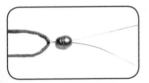

● **Tip**
Use a folded piece of beading wire to string the pearls on the ribbon.

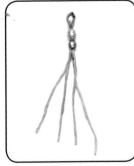

1 Cut two 5-in. (13cm) pieces of ribbon. Fold them both in half. String two pearls over the fold (see Tip), leaving a loop above the pearls.

2 On each end, string a pearl. Tie an overhand knot (Basics) on each end of each ribbon, staggering the knot placement. Trim the excess ribbon.

3 Open the loop of an earring wire (Basics) and attach the dangle. Make a second earring.

Earthy statement

Carol McKinney

1 Cut a piece of chain with four long links. On a head pin, string a 10mm round bead and make the first half of a wrapped loop (Basics). Repeat with an 8mm round bead.

2 On each end of the chain, attach a bead unit and complete the wraps. Open the loop of an earring wire (Basics) and attach the second link of the chain. Close the loop. Make a second earring.

Supplies

- ◆ **2** 10mm round gemstones
- ◆ **2** 8mm round gemstones
- ◆ 5 in. (13cm) long-and-short chain, 12 and 5mm links
- ◆ **4** 2-in. (5cm) head pins
- ◆ pair of earring wires

DonnaMarie Bates

Jennifer Ortiz

● **Design alternatives**
For earrings with a similar look but different styles, try substituting different types of chain or different dangle materials, such as pearls or crystals.

Wrapped-loop expert

Salena Kwon

Supplies

- ♦ **8** 4mm round gemstone beads
- ♦ **6** 2mm round gemstone beads
- ♦ 3 ft. (91cm) 24-gauge half-hard wire
- ♦ pair of earring wires

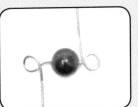

1 Cut a 2½-in. (6.4cm) piece of wire. Make the first half of a wrapped loop (Basics). String a 4mm bead. Make the first half of a wrapped loop. Make four 4mm-bead units. For small loops in proportion to the tiny gemstones, use the tip of your roundnose pliers.

2 Cut a 2½-in. (6.4cm) piece of wire. Make a wrapped loop. String a 2mm bead. Make a wrapped loop. Make three 2mm-bead units.

3 Attach a 4mm-bead unit and a 2mm-bead unit. Continue attaching 4mm- and 2mm-bead units, completing the wraps as you go.

4 Open the loop of an earring wire (Basics). Attach both ends of the dangle. Close the loop. Make a second earring.

● Tip

Use the outer notch of your crimping pliers to smooth the protruding ends of wrapped loops.

Briolette swings

Cathy Jakicic

Supplies

- ◆ **2** 13 x 18mm briolettes
- ◆ **8** 5mm twisted liquid-silver beads
- ◆ memory wire, necklace diameter
- ◆ 9 in. (23cm) cable chain, 3mm links
- ◆ **2** jump rings
- ◆ pair of earring wires
- ◆ heavy-duty wire cutters

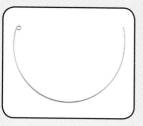

1 Cut a 1½-in. (3.8cm) piece of memory wire (Basics). Using roundnose pliers, make a small loop on one end of the memory wire, leaving it slightly open.

2 String two liquid silver beads, a briolette, and two liquid silver beads. Make a loop on the end of the wire.

3 Cut two 2-in. (5cm) pieces of chain. Attach one piece of chain to each loop of the memory wire. Close the loops.

4 Open a jump ring (Basics). Attach the end of each chain and the loop of an earring wire. Close the jump ring. Make a second earring.

Dangle, sparkle, & shine

Monica Lueder

Supplies
- **2** 26–31mm round pendants
- **2** 25mm connectors
- **2** 6mm bicone crystals
- **2** 4mm bicone crystals
- **4** 5mm flat-back crystals
- **6** 4mm flat-back crystals
- **6** 3mm flat-back crystals
- **2** 6mm blossom bead caps
- 4 in. (10cm) 22-gauge half-hard wire
- pair of earring wires
- toothpick
- two-part epoxy

1 Arrange flat-back crystals on a pendant. Mix two-part epoxy according to the package directions. Use a toothpick to apply a dot of epoxy to each flat back and the pendant. Press together and allow to dry.

2 Cut a 1-in. (2.5cm) piece of wire. Make a plain loop (Basics). String a 4mm bicone crystal. Make a plain loop. Cut a 1-in. (2.5cm) piece of wire. Make a plain loop. String a 6mm bicone crystal and a bead cap. Make a plain loop perpendicular to the first loop.

● Tips
- Use isopropyl (rubbing) alcohol on a cotton swab to remove any excess epoxy before it dries.
- Flat backs are usually available in fewer colors than crystal beads, so choose those colors first.

3 Open the loops (Basics) of the 4mm bicone unit. Attach the pendant and a connector. Close the loops.

4 Open the loops of the 6mm bicone unit. Attach the connector and an earring wire. Close the loops. Make a second earring.

Aquamarine crisscross

Karin Van Voorhees

Supplies
- **10** 4mm round gemstone beads
- **2** X-shaped spacers
- **2** 6mm round beads
- **6** silver disk-shaped spacers
- **22** faceted 11º seed beads
- **2** crimp beads
- **2** 4mm soldered jump rings
- pair of earring wires

1 Cut a 5 in. (.13m) piece of beading wire. Alternate 11º faceted seed beads and gemstone beads three times, beginning and ending with an 11º. Center the beads on the wire.

2 String an X-shaped spacer, leading each strand through half the X. String an 11º, a gemstone, and an 11º on each wire. Then string a disk, a 6mm round, a disk, three 11ºs, and a disk over both wires.

3 Pull the wires tight to align. String a crimp bead and a 4mm soldered jump ring over both wires. Go back through the crimp bead and the disk. Tighten the wires, crimp the crimp bead, and trim the excess wire. Attach the earring wire to the jump ring. Make a second earring.

Cup chain drape

Jane Konkel

Supplies

- ◆ 8 in. (20cm) 2.5mm rhinestone cup chain, color A
- ◆ 14 in. (36cm) 2.5mm rhinestone cup chain, color B
- ◆ **16** cup connectors
- ◆ **2** 15mm crystal navettes, in one-loop settings
- ◆ **20** 4mm jump rings
- ◆ **2** four-to-one connectors
- ◆ pair of earring posts with ear nuts

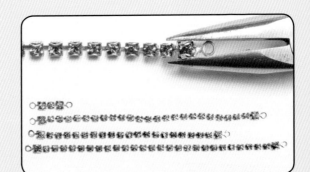

1 Cut a three-link and a 3½-in. (8.9cm) piece of color A cup chain. Cut a 3-in. (7.6cm) and a 4-in. (10cm) piece of color B cup chain. Attach a cup connector to each end of each chain by gently squeezing the sides of the cup connector with your chainnose pliers, then folding down the prongs.

2 Open a jump ring (Basics) and attach a loop of the three-link chain and the loop of a navette crystal. Close the jump ring.

3 Use a pair of jump rings to attach the other end of the chain and the inner loops of a four-to-one connector. Use jump rings to attach each end of the 3-in. (7.6cm) chain and the inner loops of the connector.

4 Use jump rings to attach each end of the remaining chains and the outer loops of the connector. Use a jump ring to attach the loop of an earring post. Make a second earring.

Jane Konkel

Jane Konkel

Jean Yates

● **Design alternatives**
Cup chain lends itself to a variety of eye-catching designs (left and center). For a similar look and sparkle, you may also consider working with channel-set crystals (right).

Leafy drops

Lacey Scott

Supplies

- ◆ **2** 25mm shell disk beads
- ◆ **12** 11mm shell disk beads
- ◆ **14** 2-in. (5cm) head pins
- ◆ **6** 10mm jump rings
- ◆ pair of earring wires

1 On a head pin, string a 25mm (large) disk bead and make a plain loop (Basics). Repeat to make six 11mm (small) disk-bead units.

2 Open a jump ring (Basics) and attach the large-disk unit's loop. Close the jump ring. Attach two more jump rings.

3 Open the loop of a small-disk unit (Basics) and attach it to a jump ring. Close the loop. Repeat with the remaining small-disk units, attaching two small-disk units to each jump ring.

4 Open the loop of an earring wire. Attach the dangle and close the loop. Make a second earring.

Kerry Melson

● **Design alternative**
Follow the same basic design instructions with different materials, like these earrings using pearls, for a variety of looks.

Figure-8 earrings

Catherine Hodge

Supplies
- ◆ **2** 7–10mm briolettes
- ◆ 3 in. (7.6cm) 20- or 22-gauge half-hard wire
- ◆ 10 in. (25cm) 24- or 26-gauge half-hard wire
- ◆ pair of earring posts with ear nuts
- ◆ bench block or anvil
- ◆ hammer

1 Cut a 1½-in. (3.8cm) piece of 20- or 22-gauge wire. Using roundnose pliers, roll one end of the wire to make a loop.

2 Around a larger part of your roundnose pliers, roll the other end of the wire in the opposite direction to make a loop. Trim the excess wire.

3 On a bench block or anvil, gently hammer the front and back of the figure 8.

4 Cut a 5-in. (13cm) piece of 24- or 26-gauge wire. String a briolette and make a set of wraps above it (Basics). Make the first half of a wrapped loop (Basics) perpendicular to the briolette.

5 Attach the briolette unit and one loop of the figure 8. Complete the wraps, continuing until the wraps touch the top of the briolette.

6 Open the loop of an earring post (Basics). Attach the dangle and close the loop. Make a second earring.

Classy clusters

Jenny Van

Supplies

- **16** 10mm beads
- **16** 1½-in. (3.8cm) head pins
- **2** 4mm jump rings
- pair of earring wires

1 On a head pin, string a bead. Make a plain loop (Basics). Make eight bead units.

2 Open a jump ring (Basics). Attach six bead units and the loop of an earring wire. Close the jump ring.

3 Open the loop of a bead unit (Basics) and attach the loop of the earring wire. Close the loop. Attach a second bead unit to the earring wire's loop. Make a second earring.

Sapphire hoops

by Naomi Fujimoto

Supplies

- **2 ½-in. (6.4cm) strand** 5mm cubic zirconia briolettes
- **1g 13º gold seed beads**
- **18 in. (46cm) 26-gauge wire**
- pair of earring wires

1 Cut a 9-in. (23cm) piece of wire. Wrap it around a 35mm film canister or other round object. Remove the wire. String 13 briolettes with two 13º seed beads between each. Center the beads.

2 On each end, string 1¼ in. (3.2cm) of 13ºs.

3 Use your fingers to form a teardrop shape with the wire. Make a set of wraps above the 13ºs (Basics).

4 Make a wrapped loop above the wraps.

5 Open the loop of an earring wire (Basics). Attach the dangle and close the loop. Make a second earring.

The chips are stacked

Carol McKinney

Supplies
- ◆ **6** 6-9mm chips
- ◆ **2** 3-4mm spacers
- ◆ **2** 1½-in. (3.8cm) decorative head pins
- ◆ pair of earring wires

1 On a decorative head pin, string three chips and a spacer. Make a wrapped loop (Basics).

2 Open the loop of an earring wire (Basics). Attach the dangle and close the loop. Make a second earring.

Lorelei Eurto

● **Design alternative**
Alternatives to these earrings are as simple as the design itself: By simply changing the beads and spacers stacked on the head pin, you can create a vastly different look. These earrings use glass beads instead of gemstone chips, for example.

Rich ruffles

Linda Hartung

Supplies

- **2** 14mm two-hole octagon crystals
- **30** 6mm Xilion pendants
- **2** 6mm saucer crystals
- **2** 4mm crystal rondelles
- **56** 11º seed beads
- flexible beading wire, .018 or .019
- **2** crimp beads
- **2** 4mm bell end-caps
- pair of crystal earring wires
- toothpick
- two-part epoxy

1 Cut a 5-in. (13cm) piece of beading wire. On the wire, center nine Xilions.

2 Over each end, string one hole of an octagon crystal, three Xilions, and 14 11º seed beads. Over both ends, string a crystal rondelle and a saucer crystal.

3 Over both ends, string a crimp bead. Flatten the crimp bead (Basics). Trim the excess wire to 1/16 in. (1mm).

4 Prepare two-part epoxy according to package directions. Fill a bell end-cap half full with epoxy and insert the crimp into the end-cap. (A little epoxy will ooze out.) Let the epoxy harden.

5 Open the loop of a crystal earring wire (Basics). Attach the dangle and close the loop. Make a second earring.

Sophisticated charms

Liisa Turunen

Supplies

- **18** 6mm crystal channel charms
- 3½ in. (8.9cm) chain, 5mm links
- **4** 5–6mm jump rings
- pair of earring wires

1 Open a jump ring (Basics) and attach three channel charms. Close the jump ring. Open a second jump ring and attach six charms. Close the jump ring.

2 Cut a 1½-in. (3.8cm) piece of chain. Attach the six-charm jump ring to the end link. Attach the three-charm jump ring to the seventh link.

3 Open the loop of an earring wire (Basics) and attach the dangle. Make a second earring.

● **Design alternatives**
The long, single-chain dangle invites design alternatives: Attach crystals at staggered lengths and a large crystal cluster at the bottom, or space charms or brightly colored Czech glass beads along the chain.

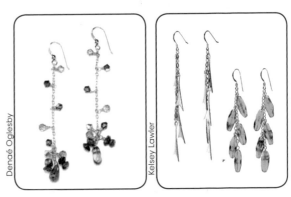

Denaé Oglesby

Kelsey Lawler

Hoops, loops, & drops

Cathy Jakicic

Supplies

- **2** 6mm bicone crystals, color A
- **8** 4mm bicone crystals, color B
- **2** 4mm bicone crystals, color C
- **4** 1½-in. (3.8cm) head pins
- pair of square earring hoops with one loop

1 On a head pin, string four 4mm color B crystal bicones. Make the first half of a wrapped loop (Basics). On a head pin, string a 4mm color C bicone and a 6mm color A bicone. Using the largest part of your roundnose pliers, make a plain loop (Basics).

2 Attach the four-crystal unit to the loop of an earring hoop. Complete the wraps.

3 String the two-crystal unit over the hoop. Make a second earring.

Tiers of joy

Karey Grant

Supplies

- **4** 42mm teardrop components
- **2** 10–14mm briolettes
- **2** 3–4mm spacers
- 20 in. (51cm) 24-gauge half-hard wire
- pair of earring wires

1 Cut a 7-in. (18cm) piece of wire. String a briolette and cross the ends above it, leaving a ³⁄₈-in. (1cm) stem. With the stem, make a plain loop (Basics) perpendicular to the briolette.

2 Grasping the plain loop with chainnose pliers, use your fingers to wrap the wire around the top of the briolette. Trim the excess wire. Use chainnose pliers to tuck the end under the wraps. Open the plain loop (Basics) and attach the inner loop of a teardrop component. Close the loop.

3 Cut a 3-in. (7.6cm) piece of wire. Make the first half of a wrapped loop on one end. String a spacer and make the first half of a wrapped loop (Basics).

4 Attach one loop of the spacer unit and the outer loop of the teardrop-and-briolette component. Attach the remaining loop of the spacer unit and the inner loop of another teardrop component. Complete the wraps.

5 Open the loop of an earring wire (Basics) and attach the dangle. Close the loop. Make a second earring.

● **Design alternative**
Try other shapes of wire components and beads, like these marquise-shaped cubic zirconias.

Briolettes take center stage

Antoinette D'Andria Rumely

Supplies

- ◆ **6** 15–20mm briolettes or top-drilled teardrops
- ◆ **2** 6–8mm round metal beads
- ◆ **2** 2-in. (5cm) head pins
- ◆ pair of earring wires

1 On a head pin, string three briolettes and a metal bead. Make a wrapped loop (Basics).

2 Open the loop of an earring wire (Basics). Attach the dangle and close the loop. Make a second earring the mirror image of the first.

● **Design alternative**
Continue the same pattern in a longer column by stringing additional briolettes on each head pin.

Berry bunches

Stacey Yongue

Supplies

- **18** 3–4mm gemstone beads
- **16** in. (41cm) 26-gauge wire
- **18** 1½-in. (3.8cm) head pins
- **2** 9–11mm soldered jump rings
- **2** 5–6mm jump rings
- **2** 3–4mm soldered jump rings
- pair of earring wires
- bench block or anvil
- hammer

1 On a head pin, string a gemstone bead. Make the first half of a wrapped loop (Basics). Make nine units.

2 On a bench block or anvil, hammer a 9–11mm jump ring. Turn the jump ring over and hammer the other side.

3 Cut an 8-in. (20cm) piece of 26-gauge wire. Wrap the wire tightly around two-thirds of the jump ring. Trim the excess wire. Use chainnose pliers to tuck the ends in.

4 Attach a gemstone unit to the unwrapped section of the jump ring. Complete the wraps. Repeat with the remaining gemstone units.

5 Open a 5–6mm jump ring (Basics). Attach the wrapped jump ring and a 3–4mm jump ring. Close the jump ring.

6 Open the loop of an earring wire (Basics). Attach the dangle and close the loop. Make a second earring.

Dripping pearls

Irina Miech

Supplies

- ◆ **2** 8–12mm pearls
- ◆ **16** 6mm pearls, diagonally drilled
- ◆ 8 in. (20cm) 24-gauge half-hard wire
- ◆ **2** 1½-in. (3.8cm) head pins
- ◆ pair of earring wires

1 On a head pin, string an 8–12mm pearl and make a wrapped loop (Basics).

2 Cut a 4-in. (10cm) piece of wire. Make the first half of a wrapped loop (Basics) on one end. Attach the pearl unit and complete the wraps.

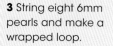

3 String eight 6mm pearls and make a wrapped loop.

4 Open the loop of an earring wire (Basics). Attach the dangle and close the loop. Make a second earring.

Facets & chains

Cathy Jakicic

Supplies

- ◆ **2** 30mm Lucite nuggets
- ◆ **2** 3mm bicone crystals
- ◆ **2** 4mm spacers
- ◆ 14 in. (36cm) chain, 2mm links
- ◆ **2** 3-in. (7.6cm) head pins
- ◆ **2** 1½-in. (3.8cm) head pins
- ◆ pair of earring wires

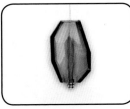

1 On a 3-in. (7.6cm) head pin, string a spacer and a Lucite nugget.

2 On a 1½-in. (3.8cm) head pin, string a 3mm bicone crystal. Make a plain loop (Basics).

3 Cut a 1¾-in. (4.4cm), a 2¼-in. (5.7cm), and a 2¾-in. (7cm) piece of chain. Open the loop of the bicone unit (Basics) and attach the shortest chain. Close the loop.

4 On the head pin of the nugget unit, string each end link of the 2¼-in. chain, each end link of the 2¾-in. chain, and one end link of the bicone dangle. Make a wrapped loop (Basics).

5 Open the loop of an earring wire and attach the dangle. Close the loop. Make a second earring.

Triple-loop earrings

Sonia Kumar

Supplies

- **6** 8–10mm round beads
- 12 in. (30cm) 16-gauge dead-soft wire
- 18 in. (46cm) 28-gauge half-hard wire
- pair of earring wires
- mandrel or other cylindrical object, 8–10mm diameter

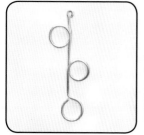

1 Cut a 6-in. (15cm) piece of 16-gauge wire. Wrap one end around a cylindrical object to make a loop. Make a right-angle bend above the loop.

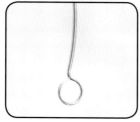

2 About ½ in. (1.3cm) from the bend, form a second loop in the opposite direction. About ½ in. from the second loop, form a third loop in the same direction as the first.

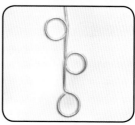

3 About ½ in. from the third loop, use your roundnose pliers to form a small loop.

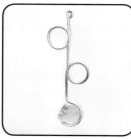

4 Cut a 3-in. (7.6cm) piece of 28-gauge wire. Center a bead on the wire and place it in the bottom loop. Wrap each end around the loop. Repeat with the other loops.

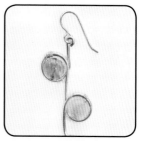

5 Open the loop of an earring wire (Basics) and attach the dangle. Close the loop. Make a second earring the mirror of the first.

Knotting 101

Kim St. Jean

● **Tip**
Use the tip of your roundnose pliers to push the beads together as you tighten each knot.

1 Cut a 6-in. (15cm) piece of thread or braiding string. String: 11º seed bead, bicone crystal, 11º, round crystal, 11º, crystal rondelle, 11º, round, 11º, bicone, 11º. Center the beads.

2 Tie an overhand knot (Basics) next to the first and last 11º.

3 Bring the ends together and trim to the desired length. Apply glue and string a crimp end over both ends. Flatten the crimp portion of the crimp end (Basics).

4 Open the loop of an earring wire (Basics) and attach the dangle. Close the loop. Make a second earring.

Supplies

- ◆ **2** 8mm crystal rondelles
- ◆ **4** 6mm round crystals
- ◆ **4** 4mm bicone crystals
- ◆ **12** 11º seed beads
- ◆ **12 in. (30cm) C-Lon thread or braiding string
- ◆ **2** crimp ends
- ◆ pair of earring wires
- ◆ Bead Fix adhesive

Ins & outs

Stacey Yongue

Supplies

- ♦ **2** 10mm coin pearls
- ♦ **24–30** 1mm beads
- ♦ 10 in. (25cm) 28-gauge half-hard wire
- ♦ pair of earring wires

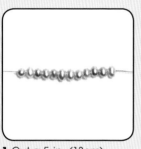

1 Cut a 5-in. (13cm) piece of wire. Center enough 1mm beads to cover half the circumference of a coin pearl.

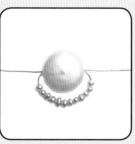

2 String both ends of the wire through a coin pearl in opposite directions. Tighten the wire.

3 Bringing the ends up so that the pearl is centered on the wire, and make a set of wraps above it (Basics).

4 Make a wrapped loop (Basics), overlapping the wraps from step 3 to add sturdiness to the 28-gauge wire.

5 Open the loop of an earring wire (Basics) and attach the dangle. Close the loop. Make a second earring.

Salena Kwon

● **Design alternative** Apply the same wire-weaving principle to double-drilled pearls, then add a dangle.

Ready to sparkle

Cathy Jakicic

Supplies

- **6** 8mm rhinestone pendants
- **6** in. (15cm) 22-gauge half-hard wire
- **6–7** in. (15–18cm) chain, 2–3mm links
- **2** cones
- **6** 4mm jump rings
- pair of earring wires

● **Tip**
Check the pendants' fit within the cones before finishing the earrings: If they're too long, trim the chains. If they're too short, make a large wrapped loop to position the dangles lower in the cone.

1 Cut three pieces of chain three-quarters of the length of the cone.

2 Open a jump ring (Basics). Attach a pendant and a chain. Close the jump ring. Repeat with each chain.

3 Cut a 3-in. (7.6cm) piece of wire. Make the first half of a wrapped loop (Basics). Attach the dangles and complete the wraps.

4 String the cone on the wire and make a wrapped loop.

5 Open the loop of an earring wire. Attach the dangle and close the loop. Make a second earring.

Hammered-wire earrings

Steven James

Supplies

- **12–16** 4mm bicone crystals
- 24–40 in. (61–102cm) 20-gauge half-hard wire
- **2** 6–8mm inside diameter jump rings
- pair of earring wires
- ball-peen hammer
- bench block or anvil
- metal file

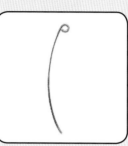

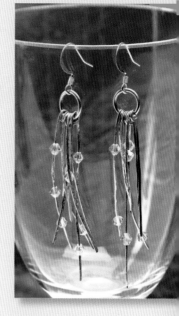

1 Cut eight 1½–2½-in. (3.8–6.4cm) pieces of wire. Curve each wire slightly. Using roundnose pliers, make a small loop on one end of each wire.

● Tip
After stringing a crystal, move it off the edge of the bench block or anvil so the wire can lie flat.

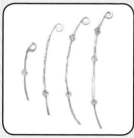

2 Place the loop end of a wire on a bench block or anvil, and hammer a small portion of it to add the desired texture. String a crystal, and hammer the remaining wire. Repeat with three other wires, stringing one to three crystals on each.

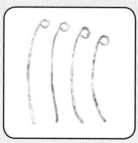

3 Place an unhammered wire on a bench block or anvil, and hammer it. Repeat with the remaining three wires.

4 File any rough edges. Open a 6–8mm jump ring (Basics). Attach an earring wire and the hammered wires, positioning them so they curve in different directions. Close the jump ring. Make a second earring.

International circles

Rupa Balachandar

Supplies
- **4** 13mm hammered disks
- **6** 9mm hammered disks
- **8** 4mm bicone crystals
- **8** 1-in. (2.5cm) head pins
- **10** 4mm jump rings
- pair of 2¼-in. (5.7cm) hoop earrings with loops

● **Tip**
Mixed metals add to the earrings' exotic feel. To create a more classic look, stick to one metallic tone.

1 Open a jump ring (Basics) and attach a 9mm disk to an outer loop of an earring hoop. Close the jump ring. Use jump rings to attach disks to every other loop, alternating 13mm and 9mm disks.

2 On a head pin, string a bicone crystal. Make a plain loop ⅛ in. (3mm) from the bicone (Basics). Make four bicone units.

3 Open the loop of a bicone unit and attach it to an available loop of the earring hoop. Close the loop. Repeat with the remaining bicone units. Make a second earring.

● **Design alternatives**
Try crystals and pearls instead of disks for a more elegant feel. Or, for an industrial look, use pebble beads.

Jill Italiano

Fan earrings

Jessica Tiemens

Supplies

- **2** 6mm crystal rondelles
- **14** 4mm bicone crystals
- 38 in. (97cm) chain, 1–2mm links
- 9 in. (23cm) 24-gauge half-hard wire
- **2** 4mm jump rings
- pair of earring wires

1 Cut a 3-in. (7.6cm) piece of wire. Make a wrapped loop (Basics). String a rondelle and make the first half of a wrapped loop perpendicular to the first loop.

2 Cut a 2-in. (5cm) piece of wire. Make a small plain loop (Basics) on one end. Cut eight 2¼-in. (5.7cm) pieces of chain. String a chain and a bicone crystal. String alternating chains and bicones, ending with a chain. Make a plain loop.

● Tip

Jump rings give the earrings a lot of movement, but you can omit the jump ring in step 4. Instead, make the loops parallel on the rondelle unit, then attach the loop of an earring wire.

3 Attach the other ends of the chains to the unwrapped loop of the rondelle unit. Complete the wraps.

4 Open a jump ring (Basics) and attach the dangle and the loop of an earring wire. Close the jump ring. Make a second earring.

● Design alternative

These gold earrings use shorter chains with larger links, and substitute one large jump ring for the rondelle unit.

Wrapped attention

Jane Konkel

Supplies

- ◆ **2** 12mm round wooden beads
- ◆ **2** 10mm gemstone rondelles
- ◆ **4** 6mm gemstone rondelles
- ◆ 20 in. (51cm) 22-gauge black wire
- ◆ 4 in. (10cm) 24-gauge sterling silver half-hard wire
- ◆ **2** 2-in. (5cm) decorative head pins
- ◆ pair of earring wires

1 Cut a 10-in. (25cm) piece of black wire. Bend the wire to mark the midpoint. On each end, make a loop and roll the wire, forming a coil. Stop at the midpoint.

2a Twist one coil upside down, forming an S.
2b Use roundnose pliers to gently push out the center of each coil, forming two cones.

3 On a head pin, string a 6mm rondelle, the center loop of one side of the cone, and a 12mm round. Bend the other cone over the round and string the cone. String a 6mm rondelle. Make a wrapped loop (Basics) above the rondelle.

4 Cut a 2-in. (5cm) piece of sterling silver wire. Make the first half of a wrapped loop on one end. Attach the bead unit and complete the wraps.

5 String a 10mm rondelle. Make a wrapped loop above the bead.

6 Open the loop of an earring wire and attach the dangle. Close the loop. Make a second earring.

Wraps & dangles

Andrea Marshall

Supplies

- ◆ **2** 14–18mm (large) briolettes
- ◆ **2** 4–5mm (small) briolettes
- ◆ 8 in. (20cm) 22-gauge half-hard wire
- ◆ **2** 2-in. (5cm) decorative head pins
- ◆ pair of earring wires

1 Cut a 4-in. (10cm) piece of wire. Center a large briolette. Bend the ends upward, crossing them into an X.

2 Make a set of wraps above the briolette (Basics). Make a plain loop (Basics).

3 On a decorative head pin, string a small briolette. Curve the wire into an S shape, making a loop at the top.

4 Open the loop of an earring wire (Basics) and attach the dangles. Close the loop. Make a second earring.

Pearl-cup earrings

Lauren M. Hadley

Supplies

- **2** 13mm coin pearls
- **2** 6–8mm round pearls
- **20** 5–10mm keshi pearls, center drilled, in **2** colors
- **4** 4mm spacers
- **2** 2½-in. (6.4cm) decorative head pins
- **20** 1½-in. (3.8cm) decorative head pins
- pair of earring wires

1 On a 1½-in. (3.8cm) decorative head pin, string a keshi pearl. Make a wrapped loop (Basics). Make 10 bead units using two pearl colors.

2 On a 2½-in. (6.4cm) decorative head pin, string a spacer, a coin pearl, a spacer, and a round pearl.

● **Design alternative**
To make a dressy variation, use silver bead caps, oval links, plain head pins, and different sizes of pearls.

3 String each of the bead units, alternating pearl colors. Make a wrapped loop.

4 Open the loop of an earring wire (Basics) and attach the dangle. Close the loop. Make a second earring.

Modern metals

Gretta Van Someren

Supplies
- **2** 10–20mm charms or drops
- **2** 10–12mm links, washers, or soldered jump rings
- 1 ft. (30cm) chain, 4–6mm links, in **3** styles
- **2** 8–9mm jump rings
- **6** 4–5mm jump rings
- pair of lever-back earring wires

● Tips
- If you like your metals dark, use liver of sulfur to oxidize the chain and findings.
- Look for individual links, washers, or soldered jump rings, or cut a few links of chain left over from previous projects.

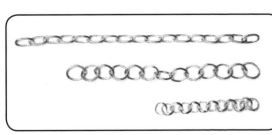

1 Cut a 1-in. (2.5cm), a 2-in. (5cm), and a 2¼-in. (5.7cm) piece of chain, each in a different style.

2 Open a 4–5mm jump ring (Basics). Attach a charm or drop and the 1-in. piece of chain. Close the jump ring.

3 Use a 4–5mm jump ring to attach all three chains. Use an 8–9mm jump ring to attach the 4–5mm jump ring and a link.

4 Use a 4–5mm jump ring to attach the 8–9mm jump ring and the loop of an earring wire. Make a second earring.

Wind up

Jane Konkel

Supplies
- ◆ **10** 3mm beads
- ◆ **12** 2mm square spacers
- ◆ 48 in. (1.2m) 24-gauge half-hard wire
- ◆ pair of earring wires
- ◆ mandrel or other cylindrical object, approximately 3mm in diameter

1 Cut a 24-in. (61cm) piece of 24-gauge wire. Alternate six spacers and five beads on the wire. Center the beads.

2 Wrap each end three or four times around a round mandrel or cylindrical object, leaving a 2-in. (5cm) tail on each end.

49

3 Wrap one tail five times around the wound wire. Wrap the other tail five times around the wire about ½ in. (1.3cm) from the first set of wraps. Trim the excess wire.

4 Open the loop of an earring wire (Basics). Attach the hoop and close the loop. Make a second earring.

● **Design alternative**
These earrings mimic the shape of a butterfly's wings. String large-hole beads on 16-gauge wire and hammer it to create a matte finish.

Gems on display

Naomi Fujimoto

Supplies

- ◆ **2** 7–12mm gemstone nuggets
- ◆ **2** 4mm faceted rondelles
- ◆ **5 in. (13cm) large-and-small-link chain, 26mm links**
- ◆ **2** 1½-in. (3.8cm) head pins
- ◆ pair of earring wires

1 On a head pin, string a nugget and a faceted rondelle. Make a plain loop (Basics).

2 Cut a piece of chain with one large and one or more small links. Open the bead unit's loop and attach a small link as shown. Close the loop.

3 Open the loop of an earring wire (Basics). Attach the top small link of the dangle and close the loop. Make a second earring.

Earring fiesta

Rebecca Conrad

Supplies

- ◆ **2** 9mm round beads
- ◆ 2g 8º multicolored seed beads
- ◆ 2g 11º multicolored seed beads, matte finish
- ◆ **4** 4mm spacers
- ◆ flexible beading wire, .014 or .015
- ◆ **2** crimp beads
- ◆ **2** crimp covers
- ◆ pair of earring wires

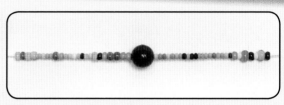

1 Cut an 8-in. (20cm) piece of beading wire. Center a round bead. On each end, string 1½ in. (3.8cm) of 11º and 8º seed beads.

Jane Konkel

● **Design alternative**
Thread two pieces of beading wire through the round bead and string seed beads and tiny silver spacers on each for a double-loop variation.

2 On each end, string a spacer. Over both ends, string a crimp bead and the loop of an earring wire. Go back through the crimp bead and tighten the wire.

3 Crimp the crimp bead (Basics) and trim the excess wire. Close a crimp cover over the crimp. Make a second earring.

Hanging by a thread

Cathy Jakicic

Supplies

- ◆ **2** 10–11mm dyed ruby fans, top drilled
- ◆ 4 in. (10cm) 26-gauge half-hard wire
- ◆ pair of earring threads

1 Cut a 2-in. (5cm) piece of wire. String a fan and make a set of wraps above it (Basics). Make the first half of a wrapped loop (Basics).

2 Attach the fan unit to the loop of an earring thread. Complete the wraps. Make a second earring.

Irina Miech

● **Tip**
Be careful when stringing the ruby fans, particularly when using the half-hard wire. It's very easy to break the fan's tip.

● **Design alternative**
Earring threads are a great opportunity to create dangles. Use a single stunning bead, as in the ruby-fan design, or consider clusters like these pearl dangles.

Ruffles & waves

Paulette Biedenbender

Supplies

- ◆ **56** 2mm round spacers
- ◆ **14** 6mm bicone crystals
- ◆ 24 in. (61cm) 24-gauge wire
- ◆ pair of 1¼-in. (3.2cm) hoop earrings

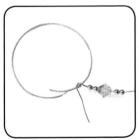

1 Cut a 12-in. (30cm) piece of wire. Leave a 1-in. (2.5cm) tail and, beginning ½ in. (1.3cm) from the end, make two wraps around the hoop. Do not trim the excess wire.

2 String two 2mm spacers, a crystal, and two spacers.

3 Shape the beaded portion into a small loop on the outside of the hoop. Place the wire under the hoop and wrap twice.

4 Repeat steps 2 and 3 until ⅜ in. (1cm) of the hoop remains. Trim the excess wire on each end.

5 Using chainnose pliers, bend the hoop's end upward. Make a second earring.

Chain for jewels

Jennifer Ortiz

Supplies

- **2** 4mm beads
- **2** 1½-in. (3.8cm) 24-gauge head pins
- **22** 4mm 20.5-gauge jump rings
- pair of earring wires

1 Open two jump rings (Basics). Attach two jump rings and close the jump rings. Make a second jump-ring unit.

2 Open three jump rings and connect the two jump-ring units. Close the jump rings.

3 On a head pin, string a 4mm bead. Make a wrapped loop (Basics).

4 Open a jump ring on one end of the jump-ring unit. Attach the bead unit and close the jump ring.

5 Open the loop of an earring wire (Basics). Attach the dangle and close the loop. Make a second earring.

Amy Thompson

● **Design alternative**
If you're not up to chain mail yet — or are short on time — try linking single jump rings like these eye-catching squares to create a dangle instead.

Just encase

Lilian Cartwright

Supplies

- **2** tube beads, up to 1½ in. (3.8cm) in length
- **2–6** 4–8mm spacers or rondelles
- 8–12 in. (20–30cm) 22- or 24-gauge half-hard wire
- pair of earring wires

1 Measure the length of a tube bead and multiply that number by four. Cut a piece of wire to that length. Center a tube on the wire and bring one end (the wrapping wire) around the bead.

2 Hold the wrapping wire at the bead's base and coil it snugly around the bead at least twice.

3 Wrap the wrapping wire several times around the wire stem. Trim the excess wrapping wire but not the stem.

4 String one to three spacers or rondelles and make a wrapped loop (Basics). Open the loop of an earring wire (Basics). Attach the dangle and close the loop. Make a second earring.

Dancing queen

Julia Anne Lis

Supplies

- **10** 6mm round crystals
- 23–26 in. (58–66cm) 0.6mm beading chain
- **10** 1mm crimp beads
- **2** crimp ends, 2mm hole
- pair of earring wires

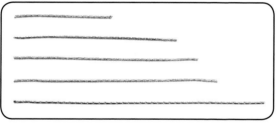

1 Cut five pieces of beading chain to different lengths, as desired. (These pieces range from 1½–3 in./ 3.8–7.6cm.)

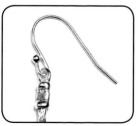

2 Gather the five chains together and insert them into a crimp end. Flatten the crimp portion of the crimp end (Basics).

3 String a crystal and a crimp bead on one chain. At the end of the chain, flatten the crimp bead. Repeat on the remaining chains.

4 Open the loop on an earring wire. Attach the dangle and close the loop. Make a second earring.

Wooden donuts

Naomi Fujimoto

Supplies

- **2** wooden hoops, approximately 50mm
- 4 in. (10cm) chain, 3–4mm links
- pair of earring posts with ear nuts

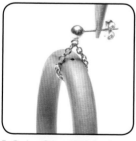

● **Tip**
If you'd like longer drops, use larger-link chain to balance the look.

1 Cut a 2-in. (5cm) piece of chain. Center a hoop on the chain. Open the loop of an earring post (Basics). Attach each end of the chain and close the loop. Make a second earring.

Rings & wraps

Jenny Van

Supplies

- **36** 3mm round crystals
- **2** 20mm hammered rings
- 40 in. (1m) 28-gauge wire
- **2** 5mm jump rings
- pair of earring posts with ear nuts

1 Cut a 12-in. (30cm) piece of wire. Secure the end by wrapping it tightly three times around a 20mm ring.

2 String a crystal. Holding the bead inside the ring, wrap the wire twice around the ring. Repeat 11 times.

3 Cut an 8-in. (20cm) piece of wire. Center the ring and wrap each end once around the ring.

4 On each end, string three crystals, curving them over the three crystals from steps 1 and 2. Wrap each end three times around the ring. Trim the excess wire and tuck the end.

5 Open a jump ring (Basics) and attach the beaded ring and the loop of an earring post. Close the jump ring. Make a second earring.

Jane Konkel Jane Konkel Jane Konkel

● **Design alternatives**

Once you've mastered wire-wrapping as a technique to add beads and crystals to hoops, you can vary your patterns for a wide range of designs.

Floral wreaths

Lori Anderson

Supplies

- ◆ **2** 1–1½-in. (2.5–3.8cm) copper rings
- ◆ **6** 8–10mm flower beads
- ◆ **6** 3–4mm round beads
- ◆ **6** 2-in. (5cm) head pins
- ◆ **2** 6mm jump rings
- ◆ pair of earring wires

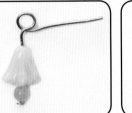

1 On a head pin, string a round bead and a flower bead. Using the largest part of your roundnose pliers, make the first half of a wrapped loop (Basics). Make three flower units.

2 Attach a flower unit to a copper ring and complete the wraps. Attach two more flower units.

3 Open a jump ring (Basics). Attach the ring and the loop of an earring wire. Close the jump ring. Make a second earring.

Naomi Fujimoto

● **Design alternative**
Try creating your own hoops out of wire to use in the place of the rings. These earrings also substitute faceted rondelles for the flowers.

Speedy filigree

Lauren Hadley

Supplies

◆ **2** 20–24mm briolettes
◆ **2** 40mm filigree connectors
◆ 12 in. (30cm) 24-gauge half-hard wire
◆ pair of earring wires

1 Use chainnose pliers to bend the edges of a filigree around a briolette.

2 Cut a 6-in. (15cm) piece of wire. String a filigree-wrapped briolette and make a set of wraps above it (Basics). Make a wrapped loop (Basics).

3 Open the loop of an earring wire (Basics). Attach the dangle and close the loop. Make a second earring.

Gemstone chandeliers

Paulette Biedenbender

Supplies
- **6** 10mm faceted cylinder beads
- **18** 4mm bicone crystals
- 1 ft. (30cm) 22-gauge half-hard wire
- **6** 2-in. (5cm) head pins
- pair of earring posts with ear nuts

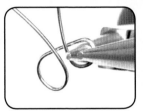

1 On a head pin, string a bicone crystal, a cylinder bead, and a bicone. Make a plain loop (Basics) above the top bead. Make a total of three bead units.

2 Cut a 6-in. (15cm) piece of wire. Wrap the center of the wire around the largest part of your roundnose pliers. Bring both ends over the top jaw, forming an X above the pliers.

3 On each side of the center loop, approximately ¼ in. (6mm) from the X, make a loop with the middle part of your roundnose pliers.

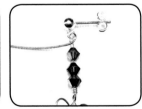

4 Bring the wires together above the center loop. Wrap one end around the other as if wrapping above a top-drilled bead (Basics).

5 String three bicones on the wire. Make the first half of a wrapped loop (Basics) above the top bead. Attach the loop of an earring post and complete the wraps.

6 Open the loop of a bead unit and attach it to the center loop. Close the loop. Attach the remaining bead units to the outer loops. Make a second earring.

Featured designers

Lori Anderson
lori@lorianderson.net
prettythingsblog.com

Rupa Balachandar
info@rupab.com
rupab.com

Paulette Biedenbender
h8winters@sbcglobal.net

Lindsay Burke
in care of Kalmbach Books,
books@kalmbach.com

Lilian Cartwright
lilian@cre8shuns.com
cre8shuns.com

Rebecca Conrad
bjc1941@aol.com

Jess DiMeo
turq2000@
    turquoise-stringbeads.com

Naomi Fujimoto
nfujimoto@beadstyle.com
cooljewelsnaomi.
    blogspot.com

Karey Grant
kareygrant@mac.com
inspiredbystones.com

Georgia Hadley
in care of Kalmbach Books,
books@kalmbach.com

Lauren Hadley
elanjewels103@aol.com

Monica Han
mhan@dreambeads.biz

Linda Hartung
linda@alacarteclasps.com
alacarteclasps.com
wirelace.com

Catherine Hodge
catherinemarissa@
    yahoo.com

Cathy Jakicic
cjakicic@beadstyle.com

Steven James
stevenjames@
    macaroniandglitter.com
macaroniandglitter.com

Camilla Jorgensen
camilla_jorgense@
    hotmail.com

Jane Konkel
jkonkel@beadstyle.com

Sonia Kumar
soniakumar92@yahoo.com

Salena Kwon
salena.kwon@gmail.com

Julia Anne Lis
beadtfriends@yahoo.com

Monica Lueder
mdesign@wi.rr.com

Andrea Marshall
andrea@andreagems.com
andreagems.com

Carol McKinney
in care of Kalmbach Books,
books@kalmbach.com

Irina Miech
eclecticainfo@sbcglobal.net
eclecticabeads.com

Lindsay Mikulsky
lindsayrose5@gmail.com

Jennifer Ortiz
jenortiz1274@gmail.com

Antoinette D'Andria Rumely
maxamarm@aol.com
cookierumely.com

Brenda Schweder
brendaschweder.com
facebook.com/
    brendaschwederjewelry

Lacey Scott
samandlacey@gmail.com

Kim St. Jean
kim@kimstjean.com
kimstjean.com

Jessica Tiemens
bright.circle@yahoo.com
brightcircle.etsy.com

Liisa Turunen
info@beadsgonewild.com
beadsgonewild.com

Jenny Van
jenny@beadsj.com
beadsj.com

Gretta Van Someren
gretta@atterg.com
atterg.com

Karin Van Voorhees
kvanvoorhees@
    kalmbach.com

Stacey Yongue
wtj@bellsouth.net
wearthisjewelry.etsy.com